TRIB

By the same author:

Idols (1986)
Plato's Ladder (1992, reprinted 1997)

TRIBUTE

Stephen Romer

for Rachel,

with warm wishes,

Stephen Romer

Tours 13·02·2000.

Oxford   New York

OXFORD UNIVERSITY PRESS

1998

Oxford University Press, Great Clarendon Street, Oxford OX2 6DP

Oxford New York

Athens Auckland Bangkok Bogotá Buenos Aires Calcutta
Cape Town Chennai Dar es Salaam Delhi Florence Hong Kong Istanbul
Karachi Kuala Lumpur Madrid Melbourne Mexico City Mumbai
Nairobi Paris São Paulo Singapore Taipei Tokyo Toronto Warsaw
and associated companies in Berlin Ibadan

Oxford is a registered trade mark of Oxford University Press

First published in Oxford Poets
as an Oxford University Press paperback 1998

British Library Cataloguing in Publication Data
Data available

Library of Congress Cataloging in Publication Data
Romer, Stephen.
Tribute / Stephen Romer.
(Oxford poets)
I. Title.   II. Series.
PR6068.O46T7   1998   821'.914–dc21   98–21431
ISBN 0–19–288104–3

1 3 5 7 9 10 8 6 4 2

Typeset by George Hammond Design
Printed in Great Britain by
Athenæum Press Ltd.
Gateshead, Tyne and Wear

ACKNOWLEDGEMENTS

Grateful acknowledgement is made to the editors of the following journals and magazines in which many of these poems first appeared: *Agenda, GRAAT* 19 (Tours), *Literature Alive* (New Delhi), *New Republic, The Observer, Oxford Poetry, P N Review, Poetry Review, Thumbscrew, Times Literary Supplement.*

'Exchange', 'Magnolia', and 'Hibernation' were included in *Hibernation/Sen Zimowy,* a limited edition published by the Book Art Museum, Łódź, in conjunction with the British Council.

CONTENTS

I

Primavera	3
How was the Night?	4
Miracle, we say...	5
Tribute	6
Necessity	7
The Last Time	8
A Lesson in Materialism	9
Ideal	10
The Other Narcissus	11
The Vase	12
Blocks & Scaffolds	13
Santa Maria della Vittoria	14
Tenacious Angel	15
Briseis	16
Romance	17
Les faux beaux jours	18
Summertime	19
Extempore	21
The Metaphysical Lunch	22
Questions without Answer	23
Under the Skylight	24
Oriole	25
Suddenly	26
Fallacy	27

II

The Premise	31
The Earth His Witness	32
Chakra	33
Buddha in Glory	34
Monumental Buddha	35
'Thy Language Perplexes...'	36
Disciple	37
Emptiness glistens	38
Nature Notes	39

III

Abruptly a wing   43
Belle-Île   44
Coleridge on Malta   45
Corsican Shallows   46
Chimera   47
Magnolia   48
Nicolas de Staël, c.1953   49
Petersburg Stanzas Revisited   50
Smolny   51
Exchange   53
After Conference   54
Linguafranca   55
Functionary   56
A Servant of the Muse   58
Hic Incipit Vita Nuova   60

IV

Shchegól   65
Sublunar   66
Laura   67
Przy-Przy   68
Of Poetic Knowledge   69
There & Always   70
Braughing   72
Dark Sister   73
A Studio in the Mountains   74
Arbbre de bhoneur   76
Pumpkin   77
Hibernation   78

I

'...who will share my discovery,
where shall I bury the gold I carry,
the ember hissing within me, if,
leaving me, you turn on the stairs?'
                            —Montale

'...My whole being abridged to this
one inclination'
                            —Coleridge

Primavera

Primavera blows across my window,
spring in every language
gusting from the aspen poplar,

flocon, duvet, goosedown-gossamer
fluff-clocks in little tourbillons
and whirlpools of the lexicon...

What can I write on her forehead
where the *dolce intelletto d'amore*
has its dwelling, the untranslatable

sweetness and modesty and virtue?
Love stands in memory,
diafan dal lume on a darkness,

flakes of snow-seed blown
into a residue, drifting now
and wasted on the brown, taciturn lake.

How was the Night?

(after Valéry)

How was the night?
At 4, I watched the palm tree
hung with a star.
The extreme calm, the mild
motionless dawn
was infinitely close
to the source of tears,
and the day came slowly
to light up
a store of ruins.
It came to saturate
things that are *all*
ruins in my eyes.

And how was the day?
Fine, golden, absent,
a goddess
I can't believe in anymore.
Despair is a normal,
reasonable state—
the only one that is.
It suppresses
what is yet to be.

Miracle, we say . . .

Miracle, we say, and destiny,
and joy and hope and repose,

when the one, necessary person
lends us fully to ourselves;

and when they've gone, the lengthening light
shows a vista of loss,

proving not that we were wrong—
only the recognition has ruined us.

Tribute

Perilous, this giving over of the self
to your unstable image, my only happiness
uninterrupted contemplation

once the minimum business is done.
It is the struggle for equilibrium
on a tottering rock of meaningless time—

as time has meaning for the saint
only in perpetual adoration.
Around the fact of loss—say it!—

to construct a grammar of recovery
based on untenable articles
and in the teeth of 'good advice':

to praise your flourishing life
from a place in the shadows
will be my comfort and my duty.

Necessity

We are scattered, you and I,
in our digital cells,

—discreet puffs of seed-down
trapped in cobweb,

congealed on gravel
or in drains,

scum of gossamer
crusting the waters:

how the great tree
turns upon itself

crested to the tips with seed
and shedding copious gusts—

such is process,
casting wide its net,

though even now
Necessity! you have no use for us.

The Last Time

I'm explaining the distinction
between *Chronos* and *Kaïros*

and the *durée réelle* that is lived in
only when your tilted eyes are on me.

I'm talking uncontrollably against the time
when you will up and go

vertical with purpose
to leave me stranded

on that iron horizontal
where nothing bears fruit or comes to pass.

A Lesson in Materialism

Our bedtime book: the letters of Diderot
to Sophie—how he rolled her out a mind—
patient girl—though all I remember now

(was it the same for her?) is the love interest:
we learned to skip the *Encyclopaedia*
and came upon that marvellous outburst

of scientific ardour, the great man's prayer,
that when they both should undergo
atomic disaggregation into air

their particles might meet and mingle
in a cloud. We too have undergone
a change; and, prematurely single,

tender traces are all I have
(being forced to disassemble you
into everything else that I love).

Ideal

I had wanted you bodily, your robust frame
anchoring me to the good things of this earth,
but already you are taken from me
by the sun, who hems you with fire, a silhouette
on this deeply shelving dangerous beach,
where you stand out to sea in the breakers:

and what is left me but some droplets
from your salty ringlets shaken out,
and specks of glittery sand fallen back
into uniformity from between your toes,
your castle engulfed already like this island
perhaps we never sailed to.

The Other Narcissus

Bare-breasted in the frog-pond—a secret
bathing-spot—and your displeasure
at my photography! Your eyes
the colour of the pond, of water

in forgotten rain-butts under trees,
full to the brim. You're frowning: by then
you had dismissed me as Narcissus
—I must be the nice one, who mourned his twin—

for here I am, crouched above the pond,
mourning you—my interrupted being—
mirrored and broken by a medium
that ripples out to everything...

In one version of the myth, Narcissus mourns a twin sister
who died, and looks at his own reflection because it
reminds him of her.

The Vase

You wanted to leave flowers
in someone's room.
I was to bring the vase.

You brought wet sprays
of syringa from your garden,
I, an ugly vase.

You brandished your blaze
like a torch, extinguished
by my vase.

You were armfuls of lilies
wilted in the desert
perfected by my vase.

To me you were always
the ideal bouquet,
I the abstract vase.

Blocks & Scaffolds

—'*Paris change! mais rien dans ma mélancolie*
N'a bougé . . .'

(*for Cécile*)

This snow on your skin is our duty to the present
falling away on every side at every second
unshareably into avenues estranged from us.

We are elbowed out by the sites and monuments
and the grand promenades of political masters,
captains of industry and moneyed contractors.

Our meagre bundle of human happiness,
or of its opposite, presumably human,
huddles at the foot of a sheer glass precipice.

Machine-washed and replete with cunning light
the crystal pyramid of the cultural state
points up our losses and our own neglect.

You met me in these gardens, a wide smile
in a Russian hat, under trees uprooted since
by the bulldozer of public safety.

These plotted saplings are not for us, my love!
I am the poison tree they carted off to burn
when the city died into traffic and stone.

Santa Maria della Vittoria

You were in Rome,
gazing at Bernini's
equivocal angel,
did you recognize
Teresa, stabbed with ecstasy
endlessly?

Ordina quest'amore,
o tu che m'ami—
but in the absence
of that order
there is only you
or not you.

Tenacious Angel

Say to the angel of the ossuary
with staring eyes and a finger on her lips,
time heals ...
It is a blasphemy;
for she is that tenacious angel
who resurrects unscathed
in the withering sun
and feeds off a diet
of mother's love and youth's perfection.

Say to the lover in his ardent chapel
surrounded by the candlelight
of remorse and propitiation
—perpetuating loss—
(his sickness and distinction)
time heals ...
He is burned alive
in the lightning
of a fresh temptation.

Briseis

Briseis! *Kallipareos!* by Patroclus led away—
Achilles drawn apart, weeping aloud to the sea—
do we glimpse, at the heart of the quarrel

something more than his wounded pride—
a sense of the unique, the irreplaceable—
my heart's darling—here, a crux—*my wife*—

that is, his slave and concubine? Something, anyway,
dogged Ajax could never understand:
you weep for *one* when we give you *seven*!

Not to mention the twenty Trojan women,
the choice of Agamemnon's daughters
and all those clanking pots and pans to boot!

It isn't manly . . . Or in the fire of his rhetoric
is it pride become conviction, Briseis mingled
at that moment with the very breath of his life?

True, he goes straight in to lie with Diomede,
also of the matchless cheeks, and there were others,
Helen among them, the dream of everyman.

But true, too, is this: when Achilles weeps with Priam,
Hector dead, and makes the old man comfortable,
and goes inside, there, in his warming bed—Briseis.

Faithful or proud or both, Achilles stands clear—
down in the kingdom of the dead
his longing for life, for any life, unanswerable.

Romance

Why should there be only *the one?*
Think of Don Juan with his list,

but also of his sadness and his hunger.
Helen was a phantom. She is legion.

Think of Hercules flayed in the shirt,
of Samson's ragged haircut,

of Dante, enslaved in Heaven,
Guardami ben, ben son, ben son . . .

of Werther and his spawn, captives of Romance,
the Terrible Crystallization.

Les faux beaux jours

(*after Verlaine*)

All day, the past has fallen
in a hail of flame
ravaging the orange harvest.

It has fastened
on the light-hearted blue
of the singing moment

and sucked you back
to what is gone,
shining in the copper West.

Summertime

All that week I woke with streaming eyes,
was it the light, or you, or for the loss
the new life brings, the casualties?

This was our retreat, our cot, surrounded
by sunflowers and tilted orange fields
and a green impermeable solitude.

The first day we swam naked in your pond
to a chorus of frogs on their lilypads.
We climbed out of the mud, drank wine, tanned

among the rushes and the horseflies.
They went for us. My vexation
registered in your sceptical eyes.

I writhed against the heat, a Nessus-shirt.
I cursed the blue, and the weatherman
pre-empted my cheeriness from the start.

I fished a string of gudgeon with livebait,
damaging them all. The tiniest swam free
at a ghastly angle to the boat.

I could do no right. You could do no wrong.
We girdled the oak tree with our arms.
It should have been like that. Yin and Yang.

You longed for your famous harmony.
I was a couch-potato, evenings were TV.
Once I shook your hand off like a fly.

You ushered a bluebottle out of the door.
Flying beetles grilled themselves on halogen,
they stank and smoked and crackled on the floor.

We concluded there was no hope for me,
not the marrying type, too selfish,
too keen to nurture my singularity,

always some impediment! From early on,
the marble certitude of failure.
Something I said, not to be forgiven.

Extempore

Touching bottom in a provincial station
one hot Sunday of early summer,
the business of meaning stalled

in the sunlight on the platform,
my future shunted sideways, a stopped clock,
or a suicide in the hotel bedroom,

I started my life from scratch
sitting on a platform bench,
talking to an affable stranger

with the whiff of drink on his breath
and a carious, defeated smile.
Waiting for my train,

I hung upon his words,
his afternoon of fishing ahead,
followed by a ramble in the woods,

and after that—
I never asked him.
He turned to the sports page, disturbed

by my access of non-sequiturs.
To him, I was unlikely, if not touched,
talking for the sake of it, extempore,

a man from the city, going home
to a job, family and friends.
Dazed with unbelonging

on the sunny platform,
it seemed I had mistaken him,
and abruptly held my tongue.

The Metaphysical Lunch

I'm lunching with a shell-shocked friend,
explaining how extended separation
becomes metaphysical, a comfort of sorts,

a way of life. The powers of abstraction
are limitless, the trick is to turn your thirst
into food and drink—I down another glass—

and to bear in mind that time, in such cases,
doesn't count. The question of her coming back,
considered *sub specie aeternitatis*,

is neither here nor there, my friend! More wine?
For trying to do right by everyone
you've been dealt a filthy hand, I admit,

de facto or *de jure*.... But rise above such niceties...
The waiter, meanwhile, is restless, and the lovers
who were leaning into each other

at a separate table have long since gone.
My friend looks hangdog. The sunny street
has emptied. Three o'clock in the afternoon.

Questions without Answer

(*after Montale*)

People ask me if I've written
a book of love poems
and if my *onlie begetter*
is one or many.
Alas,
my head grows dizzy, so many figures
superimpose themselves
to form a one-and-only, I can barely
make it out in my twilight.
If I had possessed
the obligatory lute
of a sunnier troubadour
it wouldn't be difficult
to name the one who has possessed
my poetical head, or anything else.
If the name
were a consequence of things,
I couldn't name a single one of them,
for things are facts and facts
in perspective are scarcely even ash.
All I had was speech at my disposal,
something that approaches but does not touch;
and there it is—
my heart has no depository
who is not in the grave. That her name
was one name or many does not matter
to him who remains, but a little longer,
outside of divine inexistence. So I say
until then, my ghosts, my adored ones!

Under the Skylight

Palpably, you are yourself
when I stand behind you,
my hands over your breasts.

I can glimpse a curve
of cheek, lash and hazel eye—
but you stand in a series

under your rain-flecked skylight
which is also remotely mine
from another time and place.

Yours will be counted
among those openings on the sky,
and it scarcely matters

who you are to the ghost
standing behind you, your form
a variation of the joy

that would prove an absolute
never to be concluded
in one particular light.

Oriole

Daedalio, didla-didlio—it was the oriole—
shy as your love
singing from covert and coverlet
in the broad light of morning

your nakedness and mine
our heads on the single pillow
waking to the oriole
my one and only
                    —Daedalio....

Suddenly

Suddenly I can walk the streets at peace,
with purpose, not palely loitering.
I can invoke your name among others

without meltdown. You take your place:
this was, this is, this cannot be undone,
but it can become harmless, just

the memory of a wound
that returns with a pang, but rarely.
I am no longer *waiting*. I could greet you,

and go about my business,
now that I have some business.
We could even reminisce. A breeze!

Fallacy

'Too deep for tears'—
they are those tears
and every flower shakes
with our renunciation.

All those tragic walks
all that coming-to-terms
all those returnings
with bright faces and brave smiles!

Our going down to the water's edge
our claspings of the oak
our tramps along the beach
our prayer on the mountain

—this may be fallacy, but

how should they not give back
our force as comfort,
how should they not glitter
alive with our excess love?

II

The Premise

With age there is more in less,
the spring is a work of vacancy,
of milklight through interstices

where the greens go shelving away
in their terraces and towers,
leaving corridors and entrances

breached by the glistening
that issues through them,
the annunciation of nothing

but the flight of birds through space
where space is the premise
we start from and return to, divided

between comfort and dismay.

The Earth His Witness

This spring a single spray
intensifies transparency
and shows the heart of emptiness.

Of all the forms of loss
few are worse
than loss of love by carelessness:

only the random wind
can seem at times to heal
extremities of distress,

or a hand pointing down
touching earth and teaching
the bitter grounds for gladness.

Chakra

Give a turn to the wheel, Fortuna,
(sometimes we are stuck head down
too long, noses rubbing along the rut)

—or detach the thing completely,
like this faded spring-green
flywheel I rescued from the nettles,

spoked with an elegant swastika
revolving anticlockwise out of history.
Whatever it turned or was turned by

is broken in pieces. Now it makes
nothing happen. Propped against the wall
it is the symbol of a sermon

that made the world stand still
one day in Sarnath, when the deer knelt down.
It is an obsolete flywheel.

Buddha in Glory

(after Rilke)

Core of the core, kernel of the kernel,
almond, self-enclosed and sweet—
I greet from here to all the stars
your Buddhahood, a flesh, a fruit.

Nothing, you feel, now clings to you;
your shell, expanding through the infinite,
holds the pure oil wrung from you.
There's a helping radiance from without—

your turning suns are overhead
a full and burning white—
though what in you had its beginning
shall see them in and see them out.

Monumental Buddha

Centuries before, they lopped the face,
and now, exulting in the desert,
the zealots of angelic fiat
would destroy the body also,
and ground this monumental provocation
into powder. As if their jealous god
could not abide such gentleness...

(Flowers their perfume, women their love,
and prayer—the chief of these is prayer
the Koran says—but followed up
by women their love, flowers their perfume...)

Righteous certitude blows like smoke
over granite: it cannot hurt
what never built its house
on miracle or territory or diktat;
what stopped Ashoka in his tracks,
and took the dust for witness,
compassion stirring out of emptiness...

A truth is safe in the chips of stone
flying from their hammers; they rage away,
grimacing like Mara's paper cohorts
on the night of illumination.

(Afghanistan, 1997)

'Thy Language Perplexes Me & Confuses My Reason'

A raga at dusk
means my loss,

my room out there
in the vacancy

where truth is all one
with speculation:

a figure leans on a tree
feeding the knowable to shadows.

Disciple

That our flowing away
prompts compassion,
I can understand—

that attachment or antipathy
may be undone,
I can understand—

to be equable in all things,
obsessed with none,
I can understand—

that winning or losing
may be as one,
I can understand—

that love's removal
must be begun,
I can understand—

that the emptiness
links everyone—
is difficult.

Emptiness glistens...

Emptiness glistens through contingency:
sunyatta is the word—it is strange comfort—
how the cherishing self might leak away

into the flinty soil as you fork rows
blindly for something to take root,
for a future, why not, of potatoes,

barring blight, relatively sure.
You're obedient to the force rejoining
you, as by stitch and suture,

with a familiar past, and a phrase
containing it—'low was our pretty cot'—
that nevertheless starts tears—

or with an assemblage of flowers
—japonica, forsythia—
that are no longer the properties

of lost love only—they grew there
before that, after all—and must outlast
with you, what used to be the future.

Nature Notes

Keep those yellowed notes
folded in some flowerbook,
your record of exactitudes with dates

from a prelapsarian age:
the satisfaction of fitting names
to celandine and borage

proves less a pastime
than the instinct to memorialize
what it was to feel more at home

however briefly, against the hour
of your recurrent exile
to the country of aphasia,

the intelligible face of the world
averted, its purposes
no longer your own:

then, you may happen on a list
as something forgotten,
remote as the Moghul dynasty—

how, on a certain day, *Apatura iris*,
the photosensitive purple emperor
landed on your wrist.

III

Abruptly a wing...

Abruptly a wing may open
and come beating
out of the cloudbank

and then a whole
freewheeling company
as if the cloud had stored them

in a long embalming
of ashlight and cumulus:
strangely disinterred

they swoop upriver
in a sequence
of achieved articulations.

Belle-Île

Nothing but beginnings,
the merciless polish of the beach,
something or other crawling upon it.

Compose the place—
orange room where an orange curtain flows
and swells, analogy would have it so,

as in the framing window
the sea swells and on the wall
shadowy sunlight flows:

an angel would see it differently,
colour more solid than plaster
the mirrorlight his medium

passing indifferently
in and out, above and below,
now you see him, now you don't,

caught between sound and sense
in the curling smoke-skein
where light breaks on paper

—the endlessly inaugural
never to be fetched up gleaming
real fish in imaginary nets!

Coleridge on Malta

*'. . . a wish to retire into stoniness and to
stir not, or to be diffused upon the winds
and have no individual Existence . . .'*

Petrified by the Gorgon's head
brandished nightly

and waking alone
to the usual thing—

addiction and longing
and unmendable loss—

how should the heart
not grow stony, given time,

or take a granite form
in Medusa's field

beyond hurt,
fashioned by rain

and indifferent wind
coursing over the island?

*   *   *   *   *

Yet so prompt
to delight

when he lays
self-pity aside

a lizard
or a shooting star

like a sign or wonder
quicken him.

45

Corsican Shallows

You were Silenus in the hammock—
our imperturbable Wisdom, stoical
Epicurean, with a potful of the *corse*

and few immortal longings:
our horizontal stargazer, at home
and swimmingly on the earth.

The women stood like alabaster sisters
left in lamentation on the beach.
One was Helen—*Kallipareos!*—

she of the matchless cheeks, the other
evolved into Clytemnestra
hatching an atrocious revenge...

I dreamed of a Ledean body
when we skinnydipped at midnight
drunk as gods of the golden member

in phosphorescent shallows:
all I embraced was Nemesis,
nothing but feather and bone.

Chimera

—'*Une seconde fois perdue!*'
　　　　　　—Nerval

Chimeras, firegirls, there's another one now—
blouse Bellini green, a trompe-l'œil hairgrip
on her chignon, showing a lost domain—
one of your tribe—my familiar, scarecrow,

la guigne stamped on your Russian brow . . .
No sooner seen, than translated starwards.
She would set you wandering, your orphaned
twin: the prince and princess of sorrow.

Lost and found and lost again—when will it stop?
You were looking elsewhere, at a woodland wraith,
when your chance of happiness married the baker.
My fabulous hairgrip is leaving the shop—

I bequeath her to your legendary worship.
Eyes front, head down, I go my narrow way—
but what if she were *the one*?—I never spoke!
—and so on, and so on, to the end of the rope.

Magnolia

—'Hai dato il mio nome a un albero?'
                                                    —Montale

Your magnificent Grandiflora!
Fullgrown, broadleaved and lavish.
We are gathered at its foot
like votaries round a tall Madonna.

Your teetering ladders up to God
are christened with the names of women—
the blameless ones who turned away
from the burden of your solitude.

Guide and Master, Conductor of your own
ruinous lightning, God protect us
from your beautiful theology,
worshipper of ashes, your women gone.

Nicolas de Staël, c.1953

An ochre archaeology
veined with sapphire.

Menhir-mirages of cobalt
raised out of ultramarine.

Colour from Calypso's cave
laid over fields.

Sections of Mantegna stone
carved in Greek light.

Turquoise rectangles
quarried from Byzantium.

A Russian retina
inflamed by the sea.

And when all these
loosen into sky,

a great familiarity
with altitudes

—cloud light shadow—
before the eye closed

on an alphabet of blue:
Antibes, Ménerbes, Honfleur.

Petersburg Stanzas Revisited

Pushkin's *Journal* disappointed us
on the Moscow-Pieter 'flying trampoline'—
a list of snubs and duchesses

in Rastrelli's transplanted masterpiece;
monstrous progress tarmacs the Nevsky
and gilds, re-gilds the Petrovodets.

'Europa' was off-limits, a mausoleum
where we nibbled peanuts in an alcove
and whispered in French like émigrés,

the anti-social element come home
to a new red carpet and a window on the East:
a phthisic, whey-faced girl in a kiosk

with two sad bottles of beetroot juice,
Babouchkas guarding the Hermitage
on a diet of vodka and potatoes...

My impudent love, you dragged our mattress
under the wandering nose
of Iron Felix, commissar for Private Life

and member of the gigantocracy:
he was carted away on a missile-carrier . . .
We dreamed of Imperial Russia,

revived in pastel shades on the Fontanka,
among concrete plinths and electric cable:
museum-pieces, with Onegin's armchair.

(1992)

Smolny

—'The sudden crack of an Underwood: tear out
a key and you will find a pike's bone there . . .'
                              —Osip Mandelstam

The Bolsheviks camped out
and grew bristly
near a skyblue heaven
in plaster and gilt;

the Red Guard
with baby faces
fired rounds
in the Convent Garden;

in terrible excitement
decrees went out
from the iron teeth
of an Underwood—

black on white
—the sweet justice—
—the sweet revenge—
of a world on paper.

*   *   *   *   *

Mandelstam, mind on the Mediterranean,
the poetry working your mouth
on the young inhuman hills of Voronezh:
your lived-in house, wandering window

has dried to this plaster heaven
the uncontrollable blue
flows round, with the mad longings
abolished by decree. O comrade sky!

The Smolny Institute, next to the Smolny Convent, designed
by Rastrelli in the mid-eighteenth century in Saint Petersburg,
was used by the Bolsheviks as their HQ in October 1917.

Exchange

By a series of personal accidents
I am talking to a survivor—
chatting to him, really—
about SS Hans Biebow
and his horrible rages,
about Mordechai Rumkowski
and his favouritism—
all the arbitrary rescues
from the wagons—
people networking as usual.

Oh yes, I know,
I've read about that ghetto.
Our language, our almost ease
is amazing, though we are wary
and show reserve.
We might be exchanging
office gossip,
not the statistic
which shattered
the instruments of measure.

There is something wrong
about this facility—
a presence and an absence—
a past and a pose—
though on whose side
I cannot quite tell.
We are sudden friends talking
over a divide—
and language, it may be,
is lying utterly.

(*Jerusalem, 1994*)

After Conference

We had learned to avoid
eye contact with beggars
and walked with purpose
but the pious mouthings
of our impeccable unease
where we hobnobbed
on the High Commissioner's lawn
stuck in our gullet
on that traffic island
where the maimed
are dumped by van.
The pressure building
our pockets burning
we were bankrupt
in that pause
when the traffic of India
refused us passage.

Linguafranca

(*for Arvind Krishna Mehrotra*)

God is everywhere, and satellites
beam the idiom of the global bedroom
to my air-conditioned pod. The Bengal sun
is a vacant square, cold to the touch.
In the brimming pool at eyelevel
the blue curves like the ocean's edge.
But it's snowing in Montana, and Mom
smiles whitely at the kid on life-support.
I mouth the words before she speaks them,
Honey, you're gonna be just fine—
and the girl is smothered under oxygen.
What will the linguafranca blow through next?
A Bombay broker sings the economy
as it rounds the corner and bottoms out,
and a migraine flash from Alcatel
charts the collective cerebellum
in winks and pulses. Sanitized reggae,
all night long, with the news from Bosnia,
unpronounceably remote. My heart leaps up
when the jovial London weatherman
announces Cyclone Celia, that even now
she were gusting on my face! It passes wide,
and somewhere else in South-East Asia
shanty settlements are blowing away.
I pad the carpet of this luxury
from glowing screen to ventilator.
The Fire Instructions on my door
repeat the message: *You Are Here.*

(*Orissa, 1993*)

Functionary

Bless my briefcase, bless my parking space,
bless my badges of belonging.
Where should I be
without the serious meeting
and our fluent statistician
juggling figures from the Ministry?
Here the textual strategist
beeps on the quarter
in a metaworld of flowcharts and modules
—he is at home
among the screens and simulacra;
and we have come far
to sit in council
among the abstract furniture
high above Europe's last wild river,
an expanse of plateglass
swimming with Latin names.

*   *   *   *   *

Sliding out of the concrete lot
with power-assisted steering it's home
to the Lares and Penates via
the river elegantly spanned
by a high-speed corridor
flashing with hermeneutics,
Turner's vermilion backdrop
and a lingering passage of yellow-green
in the rear-view, up ahead
the violet hypermarket, a bellowing
quarry-face of supply and demand,
appetite, technology, pleasure,
and on over rows of sleeping policemen

through the raggle-taggle foliage
to used things and the comforts of wood,
the syntax of firelight and smoke,
the philosophies of natural being.

A Servant of the Muse

Other men's visions keep him warm
in the *sfumato* of his study.
The mystics are his meat and drink.
Rain falls in upon his bed,
but what of that? *Sing, man, sing,*
he objurgates, *chew roots, survive!*
Epistles to the faithful, who stammer back,
what shall I sing? Absolutes, of course!
A crushing certitude sustains him
in a Symposium of one.
It's all an upward struggle, he writes,
after a landslide, his feet in sludge.
Come fire, come flood, (they do)—
let it all go, into the millrace!
Each day an epigram, a lyric, a broadside,
and the universe heaves into view.
Brandy and Sanskrit for breakfast,
a walk in the field overhead,
refuel his flaming verities.
He exults: *Most of the young write shit!*
As for the critics, those deriders
of the word! Traffickers in lies!
Back to Plato and his gorgeous Nous!
Sole custodian of the flame
after the Master's death, he is:
the unnamed straggler in the desert,
the unkillable exile of letters,
the last champion of the One Life.
And when it starts to fall apart,
with leaking roof and rotten walls,
when his curious hermetica
turns to gibberish in his head,
will the One in many languages
sustain him? Or will he succumb

to the devil's whisper, *neglect,*
betrayal? Will that stubbornness,
detached at last from mere decay,
bask in the pneuma of its choice?
With one Upanishad for comfort,
will he survive, naked shivering,
his face a rictus of laughter,
the rakish laurel on his brow?

Hic Incipit Vita Nuova

The great look back—and see ruins—
or forward—to one redeeming work,
the impossible City of God.

From his station on the terrace,
in the highest house of the spirit,
Valéry's constellated masterpiece
appeared to him in the night,
and I knew the value and the beauty,
the excellence of all I have not done—
This is your work, said a voice:

Silent Pound's aborted periplum,
with terraces the colour of stars—
my errors and wrecks lie about me ...
This is not vanity ... This is not vanity:

Or Johnson: *When I survey my past life,*
I discover nothing
but a barren waste of time
with some disorders of the body,
and disturbances of mind
very near to madness ...
I am almost seventy years old
and have no time to lose:

And Baudelaire, near the end:
There is only one long work,
the one we dare not begin ...
Nothing but signs and portents
sent by God, it is high time to act,
to consider the present minute
as the most important of minutes,
and to make a perpetual pleasure

of my ordinary torment, Work!
... I swear to myself from now on
to adopt the following rules
as the eternal rules of my life:

Aquinas on the *Summa*, dazzled, dying—
It seems to me but straw.

IV

Shchegól

The goldfinch chatters
beyond himself, ignites
the dreary steppe

of intervening time:
with a bob and a dart
he has come home

to his hole in the laurel,
to his nestmaking business
at the heart

of continuity where he flies,
a flashback of red
in the famished mind.

Sublunar

The aspen revives
an extended republic

sorting to its limits
the citizenry of leaves;

blue leagues higher
the buzzard is abroad,

mewing in the new régime—
or the old restored.

Only the stranger,
the millenarian comet

goes its eerie, ferocious way—
that brought the cosmos closer

for the hundred or so nights
of its companionable stay.

Laura

Could one call it knowledge?

Pace the philosophers,
I should like to think so.

The waving mass of a laurel tree,
light filtered down through mistletoe,

the close examination
of dots on your cradle quilt.

Waves and dots—
the composition of matter itself!

And all this unfathomably
amounting to delight,

delight that seizes the whole of your body.

Przy-Przy

(*for Juleczka*)

I'm about to do it again:
mistake this Polish sleepyhead
for a Leonardo . . .

Looking down into her upturned face—
God's little finger-dimple
in the cleft of her chin—

her cap of black curls
curlier after rain
bluebell clusters or meadow vetch—

her rosy ear—
the flare of her nostrils
—a lioness aroused!—

the cat in her voice,
that plosive *przy-przy*
close and remote. Her breathing.

Of Poetic Knowledge

Words cannot operate
the opening of space
when a late blackbird sings

recalling other places,
and attachments;
when a flash of high summer

breezes through an open window
in mid December where
seasons are of a piece,

and years,
like crimson in the west,
irreducible.

There & Always

A glancing visit in November
goes the deepest. A rare gleam.
Trails of crimson in every camber.

I came with a sprig from Jerusalem,
a tiny branch of expiation
to fold in your holy books. I know them,

by your bedside, Bible, a Common Prayer,
daily readings—the other bed stripped—
and the fragments of memoranda

on your table, figures, a shopping list
broken off by interrogatives
as to when and why and how you exist.

An objurgation: *To live for the children,*
who have gone. A book: *How to Get Things Done.*
The loneliness. There isn't much to go on

but you do. In my bedroom
there's a little glass of cyclamen.
I can scarcely drag my way through time.

You ward off silence. *I must get on.*
Your small brisk body has evolved
against my stalling, and in the garden

where I drown, you talk of cutting back
luxuriance. Where every leaf is holy
you are yourself, matter of fact.

So I leave you in your house, my purgatory
of mist and light and rooms.
I shall remember the birch tree

at the end of the field before us,
standing for the mind, for what I could not say,
involuted, self-delighting, bodiless.

Braughing

In the yellow room
slant yellow light
silences language with time

as I sit at this desk
now the time has come
for the monklike task

of setting down—I'm at a loss
to say what—while strangers
dismantle the house

I grew up in, the medium
I swim through silently,
so when they come

tramping to my door
for removals
I shan't be there,

dissolved by
yellow light, and the blackbird's
warning cry.

Dark Sister

There must be a name for you—
the dark one (your sister should be fair)—
obdurate, tender-proud, you have
epic persistence

in a cause that is lost.
The door bolted in your face—
he's thrown me out—should make that clear:
but it never does, there is always more . . .

You retire, sorrowing, to the sea.
In the pitchdark, de profundis,
to a ruinous cascade of coins,
you called me from a flooded phonebox

while chickens pecked at the glass:
Southern Gothic in the deep North,
that scary wailing in your voice,
what will become of us?

I didn't know then, and I don't know now.
The next thing, the new person—move on!
But this is for life,
flatly. An article of faith.

Hope is a moral duty! —though by now
a touch threadbare, otherworldly . . .
Loneliness, retrenchment—
iron rations and the clink of chains.

Love like mine is an illness,
or a principle, unhinged
from its cause, a torrent
perpetually snagged on a rock.

A Studio in the Mountains

The shadow of your thumb is lilac,
the mountains are in evening blue,
a frilly geranium on the balcony
is a highlight of vermilion, and the sun—
dissolving you, and all of this—stares in . . .

I scarcely rearrange your letter:
this latest, like the earliest, opens
with a rapt report from the palette
of all your senses, the loud song
of a redstart on the roof, and yet,

you continue, the house now stinks
of loneliness, there's a general
greyness to be got through, money
is short and love a ruinous investment,
as you put it, this time quoting me.

A tilt of houses in the lap of granite,
medieval fields puckered with gentian,
your daughters wading through scabious,
and something fierce in your apprehension
moment by moment of the changing light

and the changing time, with its inroads
of asphalt and worry-lines. Arcadia!
Winterlong, you with your fractious shepherd
clearing the track of snow, the backloads
of hay and the horses getting out,

the house you planned, a heap of rubble
with a staggering view and no neighbours.
Nothing if not hard, if not courageous!
Fragile, now you stand and wonder
was it worth it, and almost drop your hands.

74

... I compared you once to Proserpine,
wrongly, for you labour against the dark:
in that high winter field, no words of mine
perform what colour can—unfailing rescue—
a dash of goldblock among the russets.

Arbbre de bhoneur

(*for Tom*)

Darling, when you were seven
you wrote with such fluency
about the *arbbre de bhoneur*—
the tassel-haired exotic
we could never identify
outside your bedroom window.

Quand j'ai des chagrin—
all it took to cure you
was the tree of happiness.
Everywhere, the flowers
of consolation were at hand,
morning rose and peony intertwined!

Now you are eleven
and searching for similes
in a copybook exercise—
hence our brainstorming effort
to avoid the cliché
and the wearied rose

when all the impoverishment
of the arbitrary leaves me blank.
On your way to school
the plane trees stand dishonoured,
ugly roadside knuckleheads
shorn of their natural language.

*Mais il y a une chose il faut retenir
c'est un habre de bhonneur* . . .
And when you come to losing,
that is useful knowledge,
so remember, my darling, your tree,
with its hair *quomme de la neige*.

Pumpkin

The ruddy-orange pumpkin
is a cry of last colour
in the year;

its empery
is in the stifled plot;
self-seeded,

cephalic and tentacular,
it shows
rudely

through ghostlinen
strung between thistles
in the mulch of neglect.

By a chasm
breached to the West
I carry home

this engorged
harvest of slantlight.
It heats the kitchen

from Michaelmas
to All Souls.
So much for the lantern:

we scoop it hollow
and return it as soup
to the bowl of its gorgeous rind.

Hibernation

The colder it gets, the deeper we sleep...
Last night, Pascal's terror
bristled over us
scarified with points of light.

We spared a last thought
for the orbiting spaceman
abandoned out there
whose country no longer exists,

before my lips and teeth
found the soft place,
the mammal's peace,
between your neck and shoulder.

OXFORD POETS

Fleur Adcock

Moniza Alvi

Joseph Brodsky

Basil Bunting

Tessa Rose Chester

Daniela Crăsnaru

Greg Delanty

Michael Donaghy

Keith Douglas

Antony Dunn

D. J. Enright

Roy Fisher

Ida Affleck Graves

Ivor Gurney

Gwen Harwood

Anthony Hecht

Zbigniew Herbert

Tobias Hill

Thomas Kinsella

Brad Leithauser

Jamie McKendrick

Sean O'Brien

Alice Oswald

Peter Porter

Craig Raine

Zsuzsa Rakovszky

Christopher Reid

Stephen Romer

Eva Salzman

Carole Satyamurti

Peter Scupham

Jo Shapcott

Penelope Shuttle

Goran Simić

Anne Stevenson

George Szirtes

Grete Tartler

Edward Thomas

Charles Tomlinson

Marina Tsvetaeva

Chris Wallace-Crabbe

Hugo Williams